THIS IS
MY STORY

A true story of abuse,
forgiveness and God's love

MARY JOY

PUBLISHING

CONTENTS

DEDICATION

To all those who have been abused in any way. You do not have to remain a *victim*. Jesus Christ is the only one who can fully heal and restore you and give you a life, after abuse.

ACKNOWLEDGEMENTS

Thank you to Geoff and Christine Adams for your loving friendship and patience over the last 30 years. Thank you also for your help and advice when writing this book. My thanks, also, to Jennifer Rees Larcombe for her help, advice, and encouragement. I would also like to thank the Rev. Philip Bell for his help and for recommending to me the Rev. Deacon Gill Kimber.

Thank you to the Rev. Deacon Gill Kimber for her invaluable advice and helpful suggestions on how to move forward into the publishing arena.

INTRODUCTION

This book is about my journey of faith and how God has guided and provided for me during the last 40 years.

Life is not easy, and I believe we need all the help we can get. With my faith in God, I have found the help I need for my journey. God has shown me the way I have needed to go. It has not always been easy, and I have often held back, but He has been very gentle yet firm with me, encouraging me along the way.

He has also brought other people across my path to help me along the road.

We live in a cruel world. We are bombarded with news about acts of violence towards people innocently going about their business. We see people with deep anger, people in pain with deep hurts, and man's cruelty to man. We see a very harsh environment; the cruelty seems never-ending and appears to be getting worse.

We only have to look at the state of our nation to see that we have lost our way. There appears to be a breakdown in society. We see chaos all around us. The Government is desperately trying to put things right by passing legislation after legislation to stop the downward escalation. There is no time riper than now for Christians to stand up for their beliefs. We live in a multicultural society; our identity as a Christian nation is being eroded by other faiths. Why isn't the Christian faith being vocalised and defended like other religions are? Why are we not making a difference? Why are we appearing to be the underdogs?

> The Bible has already warned us about the state of the world. In Matthew 24:6, Jesus says, *"You will hear of wars and rumours of wars but see to it that you are not alarmed. Such things must happen, but the end is still to come. Nation will rise against nation and kingdom against kingdom. There will be famines and earthquakes in various places. All these are the beginning of the birth-pains."*

We are now more aware of the world around us than any previous generation, and solutions are continually being sought to find a way through all the misery and imbalance in our society. All sorts of help agencies are being set up, but so many people seem to fall between the gaps in these help areas. For one reason or another, they do not qualify for the help they so desperately need. The family unit is a very rare commodity these days; relationships seem to be continually breaking down. My family upbringing was very strict, but at least I was given a sense of values and standards of behaviour to adhere to.

It was similar in Jesus' day. There was a clear divide between rich and poor, sighted and blind, healthy and maimed. In Matthew 26:11, Jesus says:

"The poor you will always have with you, but you will not always have me."

I believe we have become complacent, apathetic, and too comfortable. We go to church on Sundays and pay lip service to God; then, we put Him back in His box until the next Sunday. This is not how I believe God wants us to be. In Matthew 24:12 Jesus says:

"Because of the increase of wickedness, the love of most will grow cold, but whoever stands firm to the end will be saved."

I believe God wants us to be living out our faith, a faith which is like no other because it is based on God alone, not on man's creation. God needs us to help those around us. He has only our hands and hearts if we are willing to let Him use them.

Just imagine the difference to our nation if we mobilised God's army, all believers who are willing to put God first in their lives. We can make a difference. An army is made up of individuals. Each individual has a responsibility to play his or her part. Christianity is an individual matter, as well as corporate. We need each other, but above all, we need a close personal relationship with God to lead us through life and touch those around us for Him.

There is a saying: "Christianity is caught, not taught." People need to be able to see what a difference our faith makes to the way we live our lives. It is no good just saying what we believe; we need to act upon it in our daily living. If people see us as being no different to anybody else, then why should they be interested in our faith?

So, how do we cope? What can we do? Where are the answers? In John 16:33, Jesus says:

"In this world, you will have trouble. But take heart! I have overcome the world."

It is not all "doom and gloom." I believe there is a way. I would like to share with you my particular journey, its ups and downs, and how I learned to cope — and am still learning, I would hasten to add. I hope that, in some way, it will help you with your journey and strengthen your faith in God and your daily walk with Him.

CHAPTER 1

My Upbringing

I was brought up in a Christian family and was the middle child with two brothers. My father was one of nine children, and his family was well known in the locality and were looked upon as "pillars" of our local evangelical church, which we also attended. My father would often speak at meetings held at the church, and he helped many people.

My upbringing was very strict. I would call it Victorian in style and a place where emotions were not shown. This eventually led to problems, so that when I became angry, I dared not show it, lest I be "told off," so I grew up in an environment of suppressed emotions.

However, apart from feeling angry, there were times when I got very excited, and these were emotions I couldn't always control. It seemed that when I was showing the emotion of excitement, I was put down. I remember on my seventh birthday, I had a party and presents. As the party got underway, I got rather excited. Unfortunately, my father became rather cross, and the next thing I knew, I was being sent to my room by my father, and all my friends went home. I found this very hard to handle and didn't understand what I had done wrong.

I started having trouble eating, and I remember my father standing over me to make sure I ate my dinner. I really struggling to eat and my dad constantly took my food away to reheat it, as I couldn't eat it cold. This went on for several months. I used to dread dinner times. Eventually I was able to eat again but I can't remember how long it took me to get back to a normal eating pattern.

My father had a lot of suppressed anger in him, and I seemed to have the ability to trigger this anger. On one occasion, he sent me to my room and then proceeded to beat me with a wooden coat-hanger across the small of my back. I remember thinking I would never be able to walk again, but I did.

My father was not all bad. I had some good times when I was older, going on walks and talking with him about any subject. We also had good times of laughter. One thing my family had in abundance was a sense of humour.

My parents were not well off, so they would save up very hard so that we could have holidays together. My father had a friend at his place of work who owned a caravan, and sometimes he would let us spend a holiday in it down in Selsey. We used to have lots of fun playing cricket and other ball games on the beach (it never seemed to rain then!). We would also go swimming in the sea. I was determined to swim to France in my big rubber ring — although, of course, I never made it!

Occasionally, we would miss the last bus home to Selsey from another town close by, which we sometimes visited for the day. We would then have to walk for miles, or so it seemed, along country lanes. My father would get us to look out for glowworms at the side of the road to keep us moving along. They were happy days with good memories.

As I grew older, I had piano lessons. I loved playing the Dambusters March very loudly, but I am not sure others appreciated it quite as much as I did. I played the piano for our youth group on Sunday afternoons when we had a service in the vicarage or church hall. I loved playing the hymns and choruses, but I did find it frustrating that I couldn't put more expression into the music. I also enjoyed singing in the church choir. I played the piano for school assembly practices and was very pleased to do this, as it meant I missed a history lesson.

I was a member of the school demonstration dancing team. We would do the dances of various countries and also dress up in their costumes. We would then put on a performance for our parents and friends. We had lots of laughs during the rehearsals. The teacher, who was the deputy head of the school, was very tolerant when on one occasion, my partner and I had a fit of giggles to the extent that we were unable to dance. Some shared joke tickled our fancy, and we were just doubled over with laughter. Thankfully, our teacher was rather amused and waited until we were able to carry on!

CHAPTER 2

Life's Challenges

Life was not without its turmoil. When I was 16, and my younger brother was 14, he developed a cyst on the wall of his brain. This brought a great deal of stress into the family, and it was a difficult time. I felt very fearful, but, of course, I couldn't show anything; we didn't do emotions in my family. It was a very delicate operation, and we were told there were risks involved. He might be mentally impaired or lose his sight if he didn't pull through successfully. Naturally, we prayed he would be all right. He survived the operation and recovered, but the surgeon said at the time that the problem might recur in 25 years. At that point, however, life then went back to normal.

My younger brother grew up, got married and had four children. He eventually worked as an ambulance driver and began to train as a paramedic.

CHAPTER 3

Christian Life

One holiday, I went with our church youth group to the Isle of Man on a youth holiday where we met young people from other churches. This was a milestone in my life. I used to get very uncomfortable in the meetings when they talked about having faith in God. The reason for this was that I didn't think I was a Christian. This was a real problem for me because of how our family was regarded in our local church. I felt that I had to be a Christian; it was expected of me, and I spent many an uncomfortable time at meetings, fearful that I would be exposed for the fraud I felt I was. I asked God into my life multiple times, but I never felt any different. So, how could I be a Christian?

One of the obstacles to my believing I was a Christian was my own church. People at my church always appeared to be smiling and saying they were fine and "praising the Lord." I knew I wasn't like that as I would feel depressed and lonely at times and not always "praising the Lord," so how could I be a Christian? What a failure I felt.

It was during one of the meetings I got into quite a state and knew that I had to find out once and for all where I stood. The bishop, who was in charge of the youth holiday, had said he would be in his study if anyone wanted a word with him. I quietly left the meeting (having kept near the back) and decided to go to see him. As I left the meeting and went down the stairs, I started to change my mind. I was just going to turn around when the bishop came up the stairs and said, "Oh, hello. Are you looking for me?"

I was trapped. So, I said, "Yes, I don't believe I am a Christian."

"Right," he said, "come to my study."

He asked me straightforward questions, such as, "Do you believe in God? Do you believe the Bible to be God's word? Do you believe Christ died for your sins?" He asked other questions, too. I answered them all with, "Yes."

He said I was a Christian but lacked assurance of the fact. I repeated a prayer after him, affirming my belief. After this, I became aware of God in my life, and I knew that I was a Christian. A peace entered me that I had never known before, and I really knew that God was there.

I never looked back from that holiday; that was my starting point. In the years that followed, I did experience a lot of loneliness, but in those times, I learned to lean on God by talking to Him as I would a friend, and my relationship with God started to grow.

CHAPTER 4

Education

After school, I spent a year in college to gain higher speeds in shorthand and typing, along with other secretarial skills. I found it very lonely at college. I felt different from those around me, and it was hard to cope with. I prayed a lot for God to help me, and He did.

After a year of college, I then started work as a shorthand typist in a bank. Being in a bank, I was able to get a bank loan at good rates, so I bought myself a car — an Austin A35 — and used to bomb around in it. I had taken my driving test when I was 17 and passed the first time. With this freedom, I was able to attend many Bible teaching conferences during the holidays over the next few years, and these were immensely rewarding. They gave me the strength to keep going. I had a lot of mountaintop experiences, and then there were valley experiences too. But with each experience, I became a little stronger.

One day, I lent my car to my younger brother, and he managed to crash it. Fortunately, he was all right, but the car was a write-off. This taught me a valuable lesson about possessions. That car had become too important in my life; my attitude was wrong towards it. People matter more than things. I eventually bought another car, but it never had the same place in my heart that the first car did. I had learned my lesson.

I used to love to hear the organ playing in church services, and on special occasions, in particular. For me, there was no sound like it. We used to sing all sorts of anthems in the choir. I remember on one occasion, we were performing "Zadoc the Priest" at a confirmation service held at our church. The organist, our choirmaster, started the introduction; he had someone conducting the choir. Unfortunately, our conductor miscounted the opening bars and brought us in two bars too soon. Our organist had a moment of real panic but stoically managed to catch up with us, and the crisis was averted. We all recovered afterwards, especially the organist who continued and went on to be our choirmaster for some years to come.

Some years later, I thought I would like to learn to play the organ, and I made some enquiries about it at church. I was asked if I had passed Grade 3 piano. I said I hadn't. My teacher died before I took the exam, and I never continued with lessons after that. I was told that as I hadn't obtained Grade 3 piano, I wouldn't be able to learn to play the organ. I was naturally disappointed. One day, I happened to share this with a family friend. This friend had built a full-size organ in his two-up-two-down cottage (the pipes were housed in his cupboard under the stairs), and he played the organ at a church regularly.

He said, "What a load of nonsense. If you have some aptitude, there is nothing to stop you from learning. Come and see me next week, and we will see whether you can learn or not."

From then on, he taught me to play the organ over a period of two years. It was difficult to practice as I didn't have an organ at home, but with weekly lessons, I managed.

When I began to work, I also joined another church in New Malden, Surrey. Not long after I had finished my organ lessons, when I had managed to learn just the basic skills, I was asked to play for an evening prayer service at the sister church in New Malden. I was very nervous and spent a lot of time practising and getting familiar with a different organ. I also prayed like mad. I managed to cope with all the chanting and other bits and pieces and felt a great sense of achievement afterwards. I never looked back after that but continued to play in church, occasionally at the main church, learning all the time and enjoying having the chance to play on yet another organ.

I then moved to the church of St Mary's, West Kensington. On my very first Sunday there, during the Notices, it was given out that they were looking for organists to go on a rota for playing on Sundays. This hit me quite forcefully, and I knew that was what God wanted me to do. I went up to the organist after the service. At this point, I hadn't played a great deal, so I told him I was rather nervous about joining the rota. Again, it was quite a different organ from the ones I had previously played on.

The organist was extremely good and talented and very kind; his main job of work was as an engineer at the BBC. He suggested a service for me to play at and said he would stay with me throughout so that if at any time I felt unable to continue, he would just quietly take over. Well, for me, that was a real challenge; I was determined not to give in and quit. I managed my first service at the church and afterwards played regularly there, again learning more and slowly gaining confidence.

It was at this church that I met my future husband in the fellowship group. He was working and living in digs in London at the time.

CHAPTER 5

Just Married

In 1972, I was married in the church at West Kensington. We then moved to Maidstone, Kent, to live. We attended the local evangelical church there, and eventually, I got involved in occasionally playing the organ. Our daughter was born in Maidstone and baptised at that church. Following her birth, I gave up work and stayed at home. This I found very hard. I had been used to working up until then and having adult company for most of the day.

I found that the people around us on the estate all seemed to go to work, so I felt quite isolated and unable to make any friends locally. I found it a big change. I had no family living nearby, either. People at our church were very friendly, but we lived a car journey away, so it was not easy to meet up. I also suffered from post-natal depression, but as I was told that Christians don't get depressed (we've probably all encountered the type of people who say "pull yourself together"), I put up with it. It made me feel lonelier than ever. But I hung in there and kept the smile on my face as best I could; stiff upper lip and all that. Eventually,

I did go to the doctor, who put me on some tablets, which helped.

Although I wasn't aware of it, changes were happening in my life that would guide me to a turning point. One of them involved the studies we attended. We would go to Bible studies regularly, which were held in small groups in people's homes. We became very good friends with the couple in charge of our particular group.

A few years previously, I had developed an annoying and very itchy rash on the back of my hands. It also spread to my arms and legs; whenever I felt itchy, I scratched. It was very unsightly. My doctor continually prescribed a strong cream for me to use. The rash would go away for a while and then return. When I was attending one of the group meetings, my friend said to me that God wanted to heal what was behind this rash. I didn't really understand what she was saying and wondered what she meant. The answer took some time to be delivered but provided proof that although we may lose sight of things, God never forgets.

During one particular Bible study, they talked a lot about the Holy Spirit. In my evangelical teachings, nothing much was said about the work of the Holy Spirit in a Christian's life. So, I became interested. After church one Sunday, when I got home, I said to my husband, "If the Bible tells me about the Holy Spirit, then that's OK."

I found an old book of my father's that had a chapter on the Holy Spirit with a number of scripture references. I settled down in the afternoon, and as I looked up all these scripture references, it was as if scales had fallen from my eyes. I had read the Bible for years but had never noticed how active the Holy Spirit was and who He was. The Bible showed how vital the Holy Spirit is in a Christian's life. He is the engine for a Christian, the source of power needed to live through each day. This was another milestone in my Christian life. God showed me the truth I needed to see and learn.

I know that before doing this Bible study, I was very suspicious when I heard people talk of the Holy Spirit, mainly because I did not understand. I know of occasions when people had gone "over the top" about God's Holy Spirit and had been very "happy clappy" and not had their "feet on the ground" and seemed divorced from reality. They saw themselves as superior to other Christians. I believed this to be very wrong.

As I have discovered, the Holy Spirit is there for every Christian to equip them for service. It doesn't mean that we become super spiritual. It means that we are properly equipped to do God's work as He intends us to do it, not in our human strength, which would not be effective anyway, but in the strength given to us by the Holy Spirit. We do not stop being human because God's Holy Spirit resides in us. The Holy Spirit is sent to be our guide, helper, and counsellor and to help us in our daily living. His job is to direct our attention in worship to God and God alone. He will also convict us of sin in order for us to keep our relationship right with God.

I would like to share just a few scriptures which spoke very clearly to me of the Holy Spirit's importance in a Christian's life.

Before Jesus was crucified, He told His disciples that He would not leave them on their own but would send them a helper.

John 14:26 reads, *"But the Counsellor, the Holy Spirit, whom the Father will send in my name, will teach you all things and will remind you of everything I have said to you."*

It is interesting to note that the Holy Spirit was to remind the disciples of everything Jesus had said to them.

We also read in 2 Timothy 3:16-17, *"All Scripture is God-breathed and is useful for teaching, rebuking, correcting and training in righteousness, so that the man of God may be thoroughly equipped for every good work."*

The scriptures have been given to us as a living word from God. This makes the Bible unique — it is not manmade but God-breathed.

When Jesus was living here on earth doing His Father's work, He received the Holy Spirit to equip Him for the work God sent Him to do. If Jesus needed the Holy Spirit, how much more do we need Him?

Luke 3:22, *"...and the Holy Spirit descended on him in bodily form like a dove. And a voice came from heaven: You are my Son, whom I love; with you, I am well pleased."*

When I first attended church with my family, as I mentioned before, we had no teaching on the Holy Spirit; it seemed a taboo subject. I discovered that it is the Holy Spirit who gives life to my faith. I can't function properly without Him.

God equipped Jesus with the power of the Holy Spirit. When Jesus died on the cross, it wasn't until after He had risen from the dead that He sent God's Holy Spirit to dwell among us. The disciples were told to wait until they "received power from on high." Jesus appeared to His disciples after He had risen to tell them to wait until they were equipped.

> We read in Acts 1:8, *"But you will receive power when the Holy Spirit comes on you, and you will be my witnesses in Jerusalem, and in all Judea and Samaria, and to the ends of the earth."*

I have found that I cannot witness or live the Christian life through my own efforts. It is only with God's help and the equipment He provides that I can achieve anything for God.

I am limited by my human abilities and strength, but God can take me beyond my abilities and give me another dimension, which is spiritual, through the power of His Holy Spirit. He alone enables me to live the Christian life so that it makes a difference wherever I am.

CHAPTER 6

Spiritual Fruit

God also tells me what spiritual fruit I should be bearing.

In Galatians 5:22–26 we read, *"But the fruit of the Spirit is love, joy, peace, patience, kindness, goodness, faithfulness, gentleness, and self-control. Against such things, there is no law. Those who belong to Christ Jesus have crucified the sinful nature with its passions and desires. Since we live by the Spirit, let us keep in step with the Spirit. Let us not become conceited, provoking, and envying each other."*

The fruit of the Spirit is referred to as one whole fruit, not fruits of the Spirit. As a Christian, my aim is to grow in love, joy, peace, kindness, goodness, faithfulness, gentleness, and self-control. How much this fruit is needed to be seen in actions in our world today to offset all the cruelty and pain people are suffering one way or another. Another description used by Jesus of a vine is very descriptive.

> John 15:1–2, *"I am the true vine, and my Father is the gardener. He cuts off every branch in me that bears no fruit, while every branch that does bear fruit, he prunes so that it will be even more fruitful."*

Here is a warning that if I don't bear fruit for God, then I will be cut off, but in order to bear good fruit, I will need to be pruned. Pruning is not a pleasant experience. It can be painful and feel harsh at times, but God knows what areas in my life need to be removed that hinder my relationship with Him. In John's gospel, it tells of where my spiritual strength comes from and the importance of maintaining my relationship with God.

> In John 15:5–8, we read, *"I am the vine; you are the branches. If a man remains in me and I in him, he will bear much fruit; apart from me, you can do nothing.*
>
> *"If anyone does not remain in me, he is like a branch that is thrown away and withers; such branches are picked up, thrown into the fire, and burned. If you remain in me and my words remain in you, ask whatever you wish, and it will be given to you. This is to my Father's glory that you bear much fruit, showing yourselves to be my disciples."*

I grow fruit in my garden. At first, I have to make sure it is well-fertilised and kept watered. After the blossom has come, the fruit sets and then the fruit starts to appear — very tiny at first. As well as the right weather conditions, the fruit tree needs the right aftercare. In order to serve God, I need to make sure I am grounded firmly in Him and that I stay part of the vine because it is there that the strength and power of God pass through to me. I receive all the nutrients I need for my spiritual health. I cannot do anything without God and need constant feeding from His word and His presence.

When the blossom appears on the tree, it needs the conditions to be right long enough for the fruit to set properly. This can be a difficult stage as a lot depends on the weather as to how long the blossom stays on the tree. Some blossoms will be lost, resulting in lost fruit. The important thing is that the small buds of fruit remaining on the tree are looked after and nurtured until they are able to reach their full potential. Before a branch grows thick and strong, it starts off as a small twig. It is very vulnerable at this stage. So, I have found it is spiritual.

When I started off in the Christian life, I was very vulnerable and had a lot of learning to do and experience to gain. I can only learn as much as I allow God to be involved in my life, and this can only happen if I stay attached to God. However, I am still vulnerable today, but as time goes on, God gives me the wisdom I need, along with the protection I need to live each day for Him. I am learning to use the equipment provided by God, namely the armour of God, to protect myself against God's enemy and mine, the devil. Make no mistake, the devil does exist.

A vine and other fruit trees have a dormant period, a resting period before they start the whole cycle of producing fruit again. I believe God also gives me times of rest and refreshment. This is just as essential as doing work for God. I have learned not to feel guilty anymore when I say "No" to someone. I do have limits as to what I can do, and it is important that I keep within those so that I remain useful to God. I am no use to God in a burnt-out state. God knows what is ahead of me. I don't — He is my pacemaker. We see this message repeated in the Bible.

Psalm 46:10, *"Be still, and know that I am God;"*

Matthew 11:28–29, *"Come to me, all you who are weary and burdened, and I will give you rest. Take my yoke upon you and learn from me, for I am gentle and humble in heart, and you will find rest for your souls."*

Isaiah 30:15, *"This is what the Sovereign LORD, the Holy One of Israel says: 'In repentance and rest is your salvation, in quietness and trust is your strength....'"*

Jesus knew the importance of taking "time out." I can say that from experience, which I have found by committing my time to God, He enables me to use it far more effectively and efficiently than I would on my own. God is an expert on time management. He also knows when I need to stop activity and rest. God knows each one of us better than we know ourselves; He knows our limitations, strengths, and weaknesses. He has given us free will to use as we choose. If we choose to do things God's way, we will be considerably better for it.

I find that as I learn to trust God more each day, He keeps me occupied as much as I need to be to feel fulfilled and satisfied that I have spent my day wisely and well. God knows what my needs are; He has my life mapped out for me, one which is tailor-made. This is made clear in Proverbs 3:5–6, *"Trust in the Lord with all your heart and lean not on your own understanding; in all your ways acknowledge Him, and He will make your paths straight."*

CHAPTER 7

On The Move

Shortly before we started our family, my husband's job decentralised from London to Bristol, which meant we had to move house. So, we started our search, and as my husband didn't want to live too near his work, we started to look at Trowbridge, Wiltshire, from where he could commute to Bristol.

We started looking just before our daughter was born in August 1974. I remember when we were looking for a house, we drove down a particular road where we liked the look of the houses. We were looking for a four-bedroom home. As we drove down this particular road, I looked at a house and quietly prayed, "That one would do us nicely, Lord." The house wasn't on the market at that time. I thought no more about it.

A couple of months later, we received through the post details of a house which had come on the market, and sure enough, it was the one I had tossed a prayer to God about. So, we went to see it; it even had a white bathroom suite which was what my husband wanted. It seemed just right and had a lovely big garden at the back. We put in an offer, and it was accepted. A few weeks later, the sellers took the house off the market. We asked them to let us know if they ever put it back. Sure enough, a few weeks later, it came back on the market. The end result was that we bought the house, and in 1975 we moved to Trowbridge.

As we were travelling down to our new house, we passed a removal van on the motorway. We wondered if it was ours as it was a Pickford's lorry. The lorry didn't arrive at the house until 4 p.m.; the lorry we passed was ours.

Apparently, it had broken down on the motorway shortly after we had passed it and was therefore delayed reaching us. While we were waiting for the lorry to arrive, our new neighbours came over, introduced themselves, and brought us a cup of tea. This gave us an opportunity to chat for a while. We were very glad they called on us. The house was in a filthy state. We had had central heating installed before we moved in, and the engineers had left an awful mess. It was an uphill struggle getting the house habitable initially, especially with a six-month-old baby to take care of as well. It took quite a time to get some semblance of order into the house, but at least it was a good time of year and not the middle of winter.

CHAPTER 8

Settling In

We had no relations living in Trowbridge. We started looking for a church to attend in the area and found an evangelical church just around the corner.

People were very friendly at the church. One lady, in particular, was very kind. As my husband was away at work from early morning until evening, it began to get a bit lonely again. This dear lady started popping in occasionally with little gifts. I shall never forget her kindness and friendship. To me, she was a lifeline in those early days.

I used to love watching Wimbledon tennis, and one day my lady friend invited me around to her house for the afternoon. She then settled down to play with my daughter and suggested I might like to watch some tennis on the television for a while with her father-in-law. She was very thoughtful. She also did a beautiful drawing of our daughter, which we still have.

Eventually, we settled down and started to make friends within the church. Things were looking up. I joined various groups in the church and was glad to attend a mother and toddler group held in the vicarage. At last, I was meeting people with whom I could speak and share!

One Sunday, my kind friend introduced me to another lady at the church. She made the comment that she thought that this lady and I would become good friends one day. What she knew or saw, I shall never know, but she was exactly right. I have been friends with this lady for over 30 years, and we continue to be close.

Things were really starting to look good. Then it happened. My daughter tended to cry a lot and, being a new mum, I didn't always know why. I tried all the usual things, but then the crying really started to grate on me. One day, I suddenly felt anger rising within me. The force of it frightened me, and I started to shake my daughter. I then realised what I was doing and dashed upstairs with her and placed her in the cot, put the side up, went downstairs, and telephoned my new friend. I must say, this experience showed me how easy it would be to take negative emotions out on my baby. I thank God He had His hand on my daughter and me.

As a result of a chat with my friend, I went to see her and her husband one evening to talk and pray about what had happened. At the time, my friend and her husband were praying for people when the need arose (they have now been involved in the healing prayer ministry for over 30 years). I was added to the list.

That first evening was the start of my healing journey with God. This was not a comfortable time, but I knew I needed God's healing touch in my life and the only way forward was with His help. More about that later.

After a while, I became pregnant again, and our first son was born in October 1976. I had difficulty trying to feed my son, especially with a toddler to look after, and I developed a breast abscess, which became extremely painful.

At the time, I was busy trying to get things together for Christmas as the in-laws were coming down to stay over the period. I went to see my doctor, and she told me that I had to rest as much as possible, hoping that it would help cure the abscess. With our in-laws coming, I felt I couldn't just leave everything as I had to get food sorted out, along with the presents. It was very difficult to find time to rest.

I regularly visited the doctor, and things were not improving. Eventually, a couple of weeks before Christmas, my doctor insisted that I put my feet up and just relax. I rushed home, baked some mince pies, and then proceeded to try to rest — while coping with a toddler and a few-weeks-old baby! I never thought to ask for help. I was too bogged down with everything.

Christmas Day came, and the in-laws were with us. I managed to cook the dinner, with help, but when I sat down at the table to eat, I just keeled over in extreme pain. In the end, my husband had to call the doctor. She was very helpful and came straight away.

As soon as she examined me, she said, "Right, straight to the hospital. You will have to have this abscess removed."

I landed up in the hospital on Christmas Day.

I was going to be operated on that evening, but more emergencies came in, so I was put on the back burner until the next day.

When the surgeon had completed the operation and came to see me, he said he had never seen such a big abscess.

He didn't know how I had coped with the pain. Well, I didn't know, either.

While I was in the hospital, more people were admitted to our ward. They had as few wards open as possible due to the holiday season. As a result, another patient and I landed up at the bottom end of the ward, and when there was no more room, our beds were wheeled out into the general rest area where the television was. This room was absolutely freezing as it was like a conservatory, constructed mostly of glass. The heating made very little difference. At the time, there was snow on the ground.

I found the food very hard to cope with. As soon as I got a whiff of it, I couldn't eat it. They even managed to ruin a simple rice pudding. As a result, I landed up in hospital for two weeks. With two children at home to cope with, I couldn't leave until I had built my strength up, so I had to eat. During my stay in the hospital, I didn't see the children, which I found very difficult. My in-laws had kindly stayed on after Christmas to look after them, but they had to return to their home sometime.

I came home from the hospital in a bit of a sorry state, but at least I was home and could eat good food. I was so weak that I couldn't even hold my son to bottle-feed him. How was I going to cope? I didn't know, but God did.

I had made good friends at our church, and they came up trumps. They came and fed my son until I was strong enough to do it. They even cleaned the house, and they brought us cooked meals. I shall never forget their kindness. I would not have coped without them.

I also had to visit the hospital for check-ups, and again my friends would come and look after the children. On one occasion, I was being driven back from the hospital during heavy snowfall. We got stuck at The Viaduct Pub near Winsley. My driver was very nervous and kept asking me to "stay put" as if I was going to run off somewhere — where I don't know, and considering I didn't have any strength, it would have been impossible. I managed to ring home to warn my friend that we were held up by the snow, and she very kindly agreed to wait until either I returned or my husband got home from work. She had her own family to cope with, but despite this, she was very generous with her time and practical support, for which I was extremely grateful.

As I recovered, I eventually got back to some form of normality. Life then settled down into a routine, and we continued to build up a network of friends.

When we joined the church, they had an elderly organist who was becoming very frail. I shared my own experience of playing the organ with her.

She said to me, "I have had enough now . You take over playing the organ."

I had a word with the vicar about this, passing on what the organist had said. I had to be careful that this lady did not feel I was pushing her out in any way — she may have had second thoughts later. Eventually, she wrote a letter to the vicar resigning, and I was asked to take over.

For three years, I was the organist and really enjoyed playing. My repertoire of actual pieces of music was not very large. I had not had much time to learn. I used to play choruses before and after the service.

In due course, I managed to find time to start to learn some new pieces, much to the relief of one particular lady

27

in the congregation. She would constantly come to see me after the service and suggest pieces of music I could play before and after. She had no idea about the pressures I had in bringing up the children while coping with a full-time organist post.

At least I had learned the "Wedding March" for weddings!

CHAPTER 9

Upbringing

After visiting us several times, my in-laws decided that they liked Wiltshire and eventually moved to a house a couple of roads away from us. This was the first time we had ever had relations living near us. They also came to the same church as us.

This wasn't always easy, but we managed to co-exist at church, and they were very involved in church life and didn't have a great deal of time with the children as they were attending meetings and going out and about for days.

I would now like to jump back in time a bit to when I was first married. My husband and I came from very different upbringings. We were both working full-time before the children came along. I remember I used to get very angry and would simmer inside when, after a day's work, I would come home to prepare the evening meal. When my husband came home, he promptly sat down in a chair to read a book. After our meal, he would then go back to reading his book. I used to mutter to myself, banging things around to get his attention, but he was completely oblivious. I thought,

"Why should I do it all? I am out at work all day, too. Why isn't he helping me?"

As I've said before, we never showed much emotion in my family; it was kept under wraps. I wasn't the sort who would throw pots and pans at him, just around him!

The problem was our different upbringings. I didn't understand this until some years later. When I was a child, my father and mother worked as a team. They helped each other when necessary. I was used to seeing my father doing the decorating, keeping the family accounts, and doing the gardening. My mother would do the chores in the house. My father was involved in our upbringing and used to play with us and shared looking after us. I remember on one occasion, I longed to paint, so when my father was decorating the hall and landing, I decided I was going to paint my bedroom door. When my father came home, he was furious that I had painted my door, but he soon calmed down when he inspected it. There were no runs or drips; in fact, he actually said I had done a good job. That was high praise indeed, as he was a bit of a perfectionist with his decorating.

With my husband's upbringing, it was a different story. His mother did not go out to work. She ran the household, doing the chores, decorating and gardening, and the accounts. My husband's father would come home from work in the evening and just sit and read or watch the television. Otherwise, he would go outside and potter around or do "something" in the garage! His mother waited on him. My husband's father was not overly involved with the children either; that was his mother's job.

As you can see, our backgrounds were quite different. When we married, these two different patterns of upbringing were brought together under one roof. I now understood what was going on. My husband was just behaving as he had seen his father behave. His father was his role model, so he couldn't see anything wrong with it. Why should he?

Just before our daughter was born, I said to my husband that I wanted him involved with his children as I believed he should be; they were his as well as mine. When our daughter was born, he did start to become involved, and as she grew, he would read her stories and play with her and then he would play with our other children when they were born.

Our second son was born six years after our first son in November 1982. By this time, I was 37 years of age, and my doctor was concerned about the pregnancy. I was very fatigued during it and felt as if I was dragging myself around. It was very difficult coping with the other two children as well. I was still playing the organ at church until it became too difficult.

After our second son's birth, I still wasn't feeling too good. I didn't seem to have any energy. I was seeing the doctor regularly, and she was quite concerned. She knew there was something not quite right, but couldn't make out what it was. I found I kept becoming quite breathless but didn't understand why. One day, my closest friend mentioned to me that there was a speaker coming to a meeting in Bath and asked if I would like to go. I said I would if I could manage to drive there since she didn't drive. I managed to get us to Bath without mishap, but I found the car very heavy to drive.

When we arrived at the meeting, I had to sit down as I felt so unwell. The person we had gone to see was a lady speaker. I don't remember much about the actual meeting, except that at the end, people were invited to go forward for a healing touch from God. I went forward with my friend, not knowing what to expect, and I felt quite nervous.

We all stood in front of the rostrum, and she prayed that God would touch all of us. Then she said something else, which I heard just as I fell to the floor.

She said, "There is someone here whose heart God is healing tonight." I knew that was me. It might seem drastic that I was falling to the floor, but it felt natural to me. I didn't hurt myself, and I did not feel any fear at all. As I lay on the floor, I could hear what was going on around me, but I couldn't move. As I lay there, I felt a pricking sensation in my chest. I believe God operated on me that night while I was lying down, and the pricking sensation was my chest being sown up afterwards by God's gentle hands.

When I was able to move, I got up and literally staggered back to my chair. I felt almost drunk and couldn't stop giggling. My friend, of course, joined in giggling with me; she couldn't help it. I felt quite light-headed. By the end of the meeting, I seemed to be back to normal. There was a difference, though. When we left in the car, as I started driving, I mentioned to my friend that the car now felt very light to drive. When I got home, the very next day, I vacuumed the house from top to bottom and wasn't at all out of breath.

At my next doctor's appointment, I wasn't sure what to say. As soon as I entered her room at the surgery, my doctor's first comment to me was, "My, you do look well. What has happened to you?"

I said, "Well, I don't know whether you will believe me, but God has healed me!"

She said, "Oh, I do. What happened?"

I told her what had taken place. She could see that I was so much better and was very pleased and accepted my story. She also suggested that I have my heart checked out to see that all was well, which I agreed to do.

This reminded me of the time when Jesus healed a man and then told him to go and show himself to the priest to confirm he had been healed. The follow-up consultation confirmed that there were no heart issues. My experience with my doctor made me feel the same. Because I was only 37, they never considered checking my heart. They probably wouldn't have found anything anyway, as it was like an intermittent fault caused by a faulty heart valve. I remember my father had had some heart trouble when he was younger, and this sort of thing can be hereditary.

The experience also reminded me of the importance of rest. When my second son was born, I found it too much to cope with being an organist at our church. It was a big commitment, so I relinquished the post so that I could look after my three children.

Of course, rest comes in all forms, and I knew my entire family would benefit. When the children were young, we really needed a holiday. Money was pretty tight at the time, but I knew I would be able to save up enough to cover the holiday. The problem was getting the deposit together in time.

I didn't say anything to anyone but prayed to God and asked Him if He could enable me to get the deposit. To my surprise and delight, a few days later, an envelope was pushed through our letter box. In it was the exact amount we needed for the deposit. I never knew who it was from, and I respected their wish for anonymity. God is good. He knew we needed the break, and He provided for us.

CHAPTER 10

Work Life

When my children were born and growing up, it was at a time when it was usual for mothers to stay at home and look after them.

I got to a point as they became older that I needed more than just being at home. I found it too isolating and needed the company of other adults. I also needed to do more than run a household.

My in-laws were very disapproving of my going out to work because my husband's mother had been at home all the time. Finding an occupation outside the household was regarded as being a bad mother. I was going against the trend.

It made me feel very guilty, but I knew it was right for me. I subsequently found that I was able to cope a lot better with the children when I had interests outside the home. I didn't become so bogged down with everything.

My confidence level at this time was very low, having been out of the working environment since 1974. I'd spent 16 years at home.

We had a little shopping mall in the town, and in that mall, there was a Christian bookshop. I knew I had to start somewhere, and I approached the owner, who I knew, to see whether I could do a few hours of work at the shop. He was very happy for me to do that, and I worked on a voluntary basis.

The shop layout was such that I could take my youngest son with me. He would play on the floor of the unit while I looked after the shop. I was extremely shaky at first and wondered if I would cope, but I asked for God's help.

Gradually, my confidence started to return. When my youngest son started playgroup and then infant school, I was able to do a bit more. These were my first tentative steps towards getting back into the work scene. Doing voluntary work, however, did not help my sense of worth. I still felt a lot lacking and needed to move on.

I was originally a shorthand typist and eventually became a secretary in the days of the manual and electric typewriter. Times had moved on, and there were now computers and word processors.

I knew that if I wanted to return to work, I would have to update my skills, so I joined a class in the town to learn word processing and took exams. Having successfully passed the necessary exams, I was ready to venture out into the workplace and be a bit more ambitious. I was still very nervous. It wasn't just the work. I was also worried about running the home and learning to fit everything in.

When I had progressed enough, I applied to some agencies for part-time work. I remember the very first place I went to was a solicitor's office. The agency thought I would be suited to this particular job, as it was of a confidential nature. I had been involved in a lot of confidential work when I was in banking.

When I arrived at this office, I was taken upstairs into a big office with no one else in it. I was then confronted with a strange-looking typewriter I had never seen before. It had a narrow screen stretched across the front of the carriage. The screen was, I discovered, a word processor. I felt as if the word processing training I had completed hadn't done me much good. However, I was given a document to type out that couldn't have any mistakes in it. I started off trying to master the strange machine. I kept making mistakes, so I had to start again and again.

I prayed like mad that God would help me get that document typed. The wastepaper basket looked rather full by lunchtime, and I was not much further forward. In despair, I went to lunch, still praying, asking God to help me.

When I returned from lunch, I thought, "Well, Lord, I am not going to be defeated by this document. I am going to get it typed." So, I kept praying for help and started off again. Eventually, I did get the document typed and felt such a sense of achievement. I was quite chuffed with myself, and I thanked God for enabling me to do it. This, of course, was a boost to my confidence.

After working in the solicitor's office, I was sent to an insurance firm in Bradford-on-Avon. This started off as filing one day a week. How the filing was supposed to take all day, I could never understand, as I finished it in half a day. I then asked if there was anything else I could do, as I still had the rest of the day for which I was being paid. They asked me if I could type. I said I could, and so I was sat down in front of a computer. They also gave me a tape.

I hadn't used a dictaphone much before, so this was also a learning curve. When I sat down in front of the computer, alas, it was a different system from the one I had learned. So, they taught me their system. This was, again, a confidence booster.

I then started to fill in for that firm during holidays and at other times when they were extra busy. My confidence continued to grow. After a while, I was offered a job on their staff, but I turned it down as I felt it wasn't the right place for me. The salary was also on the low side, and I knew for my sense of self-worth, it was important that I felt I was paid what I believed would be right for me.

By this time, I was searching the papers for jobs. I went for several interviews, which came to nothing. However, it was not wasted time, as, after each interview, my confidence continued to grow. I learned in the interviews how people perceived my abilities, which I found very encouraging.

One day, I saw a part-time job advertised, working 18 hours per week in a legal department at the local Council. I felt quite overwhelmed by the advertisement because I wasn't sure whether I would be up for the job. The job description sounded very involved, so I prayed about it and then, in faith, applied for it.

I had the worst interview I have ever had. The person who interviewed me kept a deadpan face throughout the interview; no reaction from him whatsoever. I struggled to find questions to ask. At the end of the interview, they said they would be notifying me of the outcome. Well, after that, I thought that was the end of it — nothing doing there. God had other ideas.

The next day, I received a telephone call telling me I had gotten the job. The salary was just right, as well. Then panic really did set in. I was pleased and very surprised. But how was I going to cope? This was my first big real job since having had the children. I reckon I must have worn God out with my prayers and anxiety.

I went for my first afternoon. People seemed very pleasant, but one lady was rather cool towards me. I hadn't been there a couple of days before the Chief Executive of the Council came in to see me. He was a Christian who I had seen at several church meetings I had attended over the years, but I hadn't really had anything to do with him. He welcomed me, which was very nice, although I don't think it went down very well with some of my work colleagues. I discovered some while later that there was a very strong anti-Christian feeling in the workplace. There were various reasons for this. I knew that the people in my office would have seen my application form, on which I had mentioned my various church involvements. I believe that was why I experienced a somewhat hostile atmosphere on occasion.

After my first week in that office, I nearly didn't go back the following week. I felt each day as if I was walking into a brick wall. I found that the older lady who'd been cool to me was regarded as being in charge of the office, and she was reacting strangely towards me. When she was around, nobody would speak to me unless it was work-related. I found this very hard to handle, so I asked for God's help. It didn't exactly help my confidence. I then decided that I was not going to be pushed out (since that's what it felt like). So, I embarked on a counterattack. Whenever I was in the room on my own with another colleague, I would start chatting with them and getting to know them. Eventually, I spoke to all of them in turn, and this seemed to break down the barrier which had been there.

After a couple of years of part-time work, a job in the department became vacant. It was a job I had watched another person doing, and I had often thought I would like to have a go at it. The position involved dealing with the Council's deeds, finding out ownership of land on the map, dealing with public enquiries, and entering land details on a computer system. I went to speak to my solicitor boss and asked him if I could work full time. Eventually, he came up with a plan. He asked me if I would be interested in taking on another part-time job to make mine up to full-time. I said I would be happy to do that, seeing as the job he offered me was the job I had been very interested in. God was good. This gave me very good variety in my work.

Soon after my role became full-time, the older lady in the office decided to retire. Systems were being changed for new, more efficient ones, and she wasn't happy with the changes, so she left. The atmosphere changed quite dramatically then, and we used to have a lot of laughs.

CHAPTER 11

All Grown Up

L ife was looking good again. The children were growing up and moving on. A few years went by, and my daughter was married and then my younger son was married. Lastly, our elder son got married, so all three now lived away from home.

I retired from work when I was 60. A few months prior to retiring, I committed my retirement to God's hands and asked Him to show me how He wanted me to spend my time. I still wanted to be involved with people in some way.

For several years, while I was still working, I would take a short service at our local nursing home once a month. I was also playing the organ on occasion, helping out at different churches when the need arose, as well as at our own church.

As I prayed, I had the name "Dorothy House Hospice" come to my mind. As the months passed, this stayed with me, and I felt God wanted me to apply to them as a volunteer. When I actually retired, I first applied to become a bereavement counsellor. I had a very lengthy interview and learned what was involved. I didn't feel it was quite right.

There was a lot of work involved, more than I felt was right for me. They didn't consider it would be right for me, either.

I went on the induction course, still not sure of where in the organisation God wanted me to be. I was beginning, by this time, to favour helping out in the Day Patient Unit but wasn't sure if they had any vacancies. After the induction course, we each had an opportunity to talk to the Volunteers Manager. She asked me what I wanted to do. I said I just wanted to be involved with people in some way. She then suggested the Day Patient Unit and said she would look into it. Just before Christmas, I helped with putting a mailshot in envelopes. This was an opportunity to meet more volunteers.

The manager then came back to me later and said there was a vacancy in the Day Patient Unit if I would like it. That is where I now work, and it is very rewarding. We see people who are very ill but show great courage. We have lots of laughs, and the nurses and doctors help them and work in conjunction with the person's GP and the hospital. Many make new friends, and it helps them to be able to share their situations with each other. They can also spend time doing art projects and crafts, which they seem to enjoy. Some discover they have abilities which they hadn't realised before. They can also do life stories. With help, they compile their own story with text and pictures. This is a means of leaving something behind for grieving relatives and friends to look at. We also take patients out and about. When the weather is good, we often go for a walk on the beautiful grounds.

As well as attending Dorothy House, I felt God wanted me to do more at the local nursing home, where I took a service once a month. I went to see the manager, and she was delighted. I now go there as a volunteer and visit the residents, especially those who do not get any visitors. It is very rewarding. Some like to have a chat, and others just like me to pop my head around the door and say hello. It all depends on how they are feeling, so I have to be sensitive towards them and not stay too long. I still take the monthly service with a band of faithful helpers.

There are also occasions when the residents have a sing-song, and I go and play the piano for them. We also take a carol service at Christmas, which they enjoy, especially the mulled wine and mince pies afterwards. I also help out on outings by taking charge of one of the wheelchairs. It is quite an art steering these chairs, and on my first occasion, much to my occupant's delight, I nearly demolished a row of neatly arranged shoes on the bottom row of a display in Marks & Spencer! It gave us a good laugh.

From when I was a young girl, I had wanted to become a nurse. I always felt within me a desire to help people in some way. It seems that after all these years, God has opened up a way for me to fulfil that desire, not as a nurse, but by giving me an opportunity to care for others.

I am still being given opportunities to play the organ and help out at local churches when the need arises for services, funerals, and occasional weddings.

CHAPTER 12

Healing

As I mentioned earlier, my family background comprised, in part, suppressed emotions. God saw it was time for me to be healed and set free from the chains of the past.

My first time being prayed for was about my anger, which I saw later was covering a lot of other emotions, but the anger had to be dealt with first.

I visited my friends again, and we waited on God. I felt the need to be able to squeeze something. I was given a pillow, which I was able to squeeze to help me get in touch with my anger. As I squeezed the pillow, I felt the anger again, and as it came up, I was able to let it out. The pillow got a real beating, but boy, did I start to feel better, although rather exhausted. The anger had to come out, and I was able to let it out in a controlled and safe environment. The only harm done was when I opened my eyes and looked around, there were all these feathers flying around in the air. I had shredded the cover of the pillow so finely that all the innards of the pillow came out. At least we were able to laugh about it. God was very gracious. But this showed me how strong and dangerous my suppressed anger was.

Over time, I gradually released all the anger within me until it was all spent and cleansed away by prayer. But what was behind the anger? I didn't become angry without a reason or reasons. Over a period of years, I have been prayed for to uncover what was behind the anger. I had a lot of anger towards my parents, and I had to be willing to let go of it and give it to God. I had to forgive my parents. It wasn't easy, but with God's help, I managed it. So, the healing process continued.

As I received my healing gradually over the years, so my energy levels improved. It takes an enormous amount of energy to keep our emotions suppressed. It also made me feel quite unwell at times. It occurred to me later that these ministry sessions were spaced out over time. God knows how much we can cope with at any one time. There were times when it seemed just too much, but God knew better, and of course, He was always right.

God was always there with me, and I felt safe in that knowledge. Another interesting fact was that the rash I had on my hands and arms started to disappear and heal up. What my friend in Maidstone said all those years ago was right. As I received God's healing for my "dis-ease" within, so He healed my diseased hands and arms. The rash appeared to be an outward sign of my inner dis-ease.

I was never able to share what God had done for me with my parents. They just would not have understood, and it would have caused more trouble than healing.

CHAPTER 13

Memories

I had a lot of laughs with my mother over the years; she had a good sense of humour. We used to go to the C&A shop and try on the hats, posing in front of the mirrors. We would become quite hysterical with laughter, looking at the sight of ourselves. Yes, there were times of laughter, too.

My mother retired when she was 60, having worked for many years for the electricity board. My father was also now retired. We didn't see much of them at this time. She had always had trouble with being overweight and had tried for years to lose some but was unsuccessful.

As time passed, she became unwell and in a great deal of pain, but she still wouldn't go to the doctor. Having had previous bad experiences with doctors, she refused to see one. At that time, I was married with three young children. My youngest was around two years old, so when my father asked me to go to see her, I took him with me.

My father wanted her to see the doctor, but she wouldn't go, so he asked me to persuade her. I had a talk with my mum, and eventually, she agreed to get medical advice. She was immediately rushed to the hospital and operated on. They discovered she had ovarian cancer, and she died six months later.

When she was ill in the hospital, she called me to her bedside and asked me to keep an eye on my dad. I said I would. She then returned home, where she died three months later.

My husband and I managed to get down to see her before she died to say our goodbyes. My husband and I left the children with the in-laws and arrived at my parent's home at around 1 p.m. My mother had been unconscious most of the time. Shortly after we arrived, she suddenly opened her eyes, took a long look at me, and then closed her eyes again. She never regained consciousness after that. It was as if she was waiting to see me. At 5:30 that evening, she died peacefully, and I remember looking out of the window and seeing a beautiful sunset, which seemed rather fitting.

Unfortunately, after my mother's death, my father didn't want anything to do with me or my family. This made it very difficult, as my mother had asked me to keep an eye on him. I used to telephone him on a regular basis to see that he was all right, but he started to be very unpleasant on the telephone. I found this very hurtful. Every time I rang him, I was coping with rejection from him. In the end, I had to stop telephoning him because it became too damaging to me. I had to forgive him and managed to do so eventually, with God's help. This situation prevailed until the day of his death.

The children found this very hard and hurtful. My father cut himself off from everyone, although he did allow my elder brother and his wife to see him very occasionally. He even turned away his own brother, who tried to reach him. He was also quite rude to his neighbours. This was sad because they kindly kept an eye on him.

One day, they noticed he hadn't taken in his milk. They rang the police, and together they went into the bungalow. Dad was lying on the floor in the living room. The doctor said he wouldn't have suffered; he just collapsed and died. I was very thankful for this, as I didn't like the thought of him having a lingering death with no one around to care for him.

CHAPTER 14

Goodbye

As predicted by the surgeon, my younger brother became ill again, and yes, it was actually 25 years later, as the surgeon had said. He developed a cyst on his pituitary gland. He was back in hospital and underwent three major operations in six months. The nurses and doctors were amazed at how he survived this. He then had two attacks of meningitis. During the last attack, he was rushed to the hospital, but they were unable to raise his blood pressure. I was very thankful that they couldn't revive him because he had suffered so much, and his quality of life was not at all good.

He eventually died at age 43. I went to see him a couple of months before he died. I knew I was saying my goodbyes. As our conversation came to a close, in my mind, I had a picture of him stepping onto a wooden bridge, turning to look at me, and then walking over the bridge. I shall never forget the memory. It was one of peace, and I knew that he had arrived safely in God's hands, where there would be no more sickness or disease for him but a new heavenly body.

I was glad that my brother did not die before my mother because I don't think she would have coped well. My father did not attend the funeral. He remained cut off from the family, which people found very hard to understand.

CHAPTER 15

Process

After a lot of prayers and careful consideration, we felt God was leading us to attend another church in Trowbridge, having been at ours for about 18 years. That's when I encountered more difficulties.

I had been brought up all my life in an evangelical church environment. Although I wasn't particularly comfortable in it, it was all I knew at the time. Going to this new church felt like a very big step into the unknown. Leaving a church environment which I had always known, gave me a real sense of insecurity, but now God was moving me out of my comfort zone into a new area for my life. "What next?" I thought!

When we started going to the church, the people were very friendly and welcoming to us. Our close friends had also moved to the church at the same time. The church was a little high (much higher than the evangelical!). Meaning, more rituals were undertaken in the church, but I didn't really mind that. They had candles. Wow! Although the evangelical church did not go with candles, I really liked them and felt they were an excellent symbol of God's light. Perhaps a bit of high churchmanship was lurking in me somewhere.

As we settled down in the church, I started to feel very lonely and cut off again. I couldn't understand why. People were very friendly, so what was wrong? After much prayer and seeking God, I saw a picture of myself encased in a steel case which completely covered me. God showed me that the case represented the evangelical influence on my life. It was like living in a straitjacket. I had become a person God had not intended me to be. God showed me that all the wrong attitudes and influences I had been brought up with were making up this straitjacket.

It was a very painful process. Over a period of time, I had to be willing to surrender to God all my wrong attitudes. This took time, but gradually, as God highlighted my wrong attitudes, I surrendered them to Him and began to feel a lot freer and not so lonely. I was beginning to relate to people better because God took away my judgmental thoughts and my pride. I started becoming the person God had intended me to be.

The church choir consisted of boys and men, but later on, it changed to both men and women, so I was able to join. Eventually, after many years of not playing, I had the opportunity to play the organ again. I now help out occasionally at several churches. I believe God has given me a gift in organ playing, which He wants me to keep using. God's hand has been on me over the years. He has given me the opportunity to develop my musical gift in organ playing. I always pray that God's spirit will move through my playing and touch others for Him.

CHAPTER 16

Words From God

For some areas of my healing, I went away for weekend retreats, and through the people who ministered to me, I was given words from God that were of great comfort and encouragement to me. I knew God's hand was on me and that He had a purpose for my life. Throughout the entire ministry by God, my walk with Him was gaining in confidence and strength. He was and is my dependable friend, guide and counsellor, and I knew that whatever else happened, I would never be alone because He would always be there. He would be with me in the dark places where no one else could go with me.

One of the many words given to me by God through the ministry team (in 1993) was Isaiah 61:3:7, which reads:

> *"...and provide for those who grieve in Zion — to bestow on them a crown of beauty instead of ashes, the oil of gladness instead of mourning, and a garment of praise instead of a spirit of despair. They*

will be called oaks of righteousness, a planting of the Lord for the display of His splendour.

"Instead of their shame, my people will receive a double portion, and instead of disgrace, they will rejoice in their inheritance; and so they will inherit a double portion in their land, and everlasting joy will be theirs."

I would like to quote a couple more words which were given to me during a ministry session in 1996.

Psalm 34:4–6, *"I sought the Lord, and He answered me; He delivered me from all my fears. Those who look to Him are radiant; their faces are never covered with shame. This poor man called, and the Lord heard him; He saved him out of all his troubles."*

Psalm 25:1–3, *"To you, O Lord, I lift up my soul; in you I trust, O my God. Do not let me be put to shame, nor let my enemies triumph over me. No one whose hope is in you will ever be put to shame..."*

These words given to me were of great comfort, but I didn't quite understand the words about "shame" until a few years later.

I have found in God's goodness towards me that He only brings me face-to-face with past hurts when I am strong enough in Him to deal with them. This next hurt is a case in point. After all these years and many hours of receiving God's grace and healing in ministry, I found my thoughts wandering back to when I was a small child, and I started to feel uneasy.

I felt God was asking me to look at something, and so a memory I had suppressed for over 50 years was brought back to me. I knew something bad had happened when I was very young, and so I sought out my close friends, who I trusted, to pray with me.

I did not find it easy, but with God's help, I was able to face the memory of being sexually abused by my father when I was five years old. At the time, I remember trying to tell my mother, who seemed very afraid, and she wouldn't believe me. As I grew up, I had wondered why I felt different from everybody else. I felt apart from others and awkward. I didn't know who I really was. I felt very insecure. I had difficulty relating to people. I invited God into the situation and received His healing. But that wasn't the end of it. I had to be able to forgive my father. It took me quite a long time. Over time, I had to continually keep coming back to God, saying I forgave my father and asking God to help me to mean it from the heart. When I managed this, I came into freedom.

After this ministry, I started calling God my heavenly Father and have done so ever since. I am a daughter of the heavenly King. God is my Father as well as my friend.

It was after this particular ministry that I understood a lot of the words which God had given me previously. They made sense, but He knew that.

CHAPTER 17

Forgiveness

This brings me to another topic. The thread that has run through my life has been the thread of forgiving. I have had to learn to forgive. When Jesus was dying on the cross, He said, *"Father, forgive them..."*

> Jesus also said in Mark 11:25, *"And when you stand praying, if you hold anything against anyone, forgive him, so that your Father in heaven may forgive you your sins."*

Forgiveness is one of the hardest things to do. When we are hurt by someone, we want to hit out at them and cause them to hurt. But does this make us feel any better? I believe that when we do this, we stay joined to that person in that hurt, and we feed our own hurt by hurting them. We perpetuate the hurt, and we become bogged down by it. As a result, we come into bondage with that person. We hear on the news about people who say they can never forgive.

The person they are damaging the most by not forgiving is themselves, not the perpetrator of the hurt to them.

How are we hurting ourselves by not forgiving? The hurt we hold on to eats into us, making us ill and bitter, and we become a person to be avoided by others.

Jesus knew what He was talking about when He said, *"Father, forgive them."* God knows that in order for us to lead healthy, balanced lives and become the person He wants us to be, we need to forgive those who wrong us, for our health's sake, but not only for that reason. Jesus also said, *"If you hold anything against anyone, forgive them, so that your Father in heaven may forgive you your sins."* (Mark 11:25)

God's forgiveness to us is conditional on us forgiving others who have wronged us. What right do we have not to forgive others who sin against us if God is willing to forgive us our sins? We see the price of our sin in that God let go of His only Son, Jesus Christ, and turned His back on Him when He was on the cross. Why? Because Jesus was carrying my sin and yours, and God, being a holy God, cannot look on sin and accept it.

How God must have suffered to have to turn His back on His only Son; what agony He must have felt at the separation. The sufferings we go through can only teach us in a small way what suffering God felt and what Jesus suffered for us in order that we may be ransomed, healed, restored, and forgiven. This is why God understands our pain. He understands my pain and brings His healing touch to restore me.

As Christians, we have no right not to forgive those who "trespass against us," as this is the very foundation of our Christian faith. It is only through forgiveness that we are restored to God, through Jesus Christ.

CHAPTER 18

Emotions

I have spent years working hard at forgiving, and it was only a short while ago that I actually understood how to go about it more effectively and quickly.

The first emotion I have had to deal with is my pride. It is pride that stops me from forgiving. I don't want to be seen to be overcome by the perpetrator. I must win, and I would do that by hitting back. Because I was proud, I was unwilling to bend to the will of God. Jesus said, "Forgive." I said, "Not yet, Lord. I just want to take a few more swipes at him/her first."

I have to be willing to let go of my pride by handing it over to God to be cleansed away.

Secondly, it's a question of "willingness." Once I have laid aside my pride, I come to the matter of my will. I do not believe that, in my natural state, I am able to fully forgive. I believe I need God's help. I have found that forgiving others is more a question of my saying to God, "God, I am willing to forgive this person for hurting me so badly. Please give me the ability to forgive them." I am showing God my willingness to let go and release the other person from my unforgiveness. I have found that God then gives me the ability to forgive that person from my heart. God deals with my heart once I have given Him permission to do so. I still have the free choice here.

I start off forgiving with my mind by telling God I am willing to forgive. This is then followed by "heart forgiveness," which God gives me. It is about submitting my will to God so that He can do the work within me.

It has taken me a long time to learn this about forgiveness, but I see that God has made it clear that if we do not forgive others, we will not be forgiven.

My journey of forgiving continues because I am not perfect, and we do not live in a perfect world. There are going to be times in the future when I will need to forgive. I have found that as I have forgiven people who have hurt me, so my faith has become stronger, I am learning more about God, and I am walking in greater inner freedom than I have known before.

CHAPTER 19

Great Is God's Faithfulness

L amentations 3:22–23, *"Because of the Lord's great love, we are not consumed, for His compassions never fail. They are new every morning; great is your faithfulness."*

These scriptures were given to me by the ministry team who prayed for me in 1996. That was ten years ago.

My favourite hymn is "Great is Thy Faithfulness," which is based on these scriptures. Throughout my life thus far, God has proved His complete dependability to me. God has been faithful to me; He has shown me great compassion in the healing He has brought me.

As I continue on my Christian journey, I have found that God's mercies are new every morning. He gives me satisfaction, a sense of purpose, and the strength to cope with each day. I never know what a day may bring, but I know that God has a purpose for me in each day with whomever I happen to meet or whatever I do.

Another thing I have found is that as I write this book, remembering the past, I can write about it with a spirit of thankfulness. God has done so much for me, for which I give Him praise and thanks. He has made my life worthwhile. He is my heavenly Father, and that gives me a security within that nothing else can. I find I can remember the past without pain or any other negative feeling. This is the beauty of God's healing grace. It is only when we remember our past with pain and anger that it does us harm. God enables me to remember in a way that is not damaging to me.

People say we should forget the past, but I don't agree. We can learn a lot from our past, and also, as we look back, we can see how far we have travelled in our walk with God and how much God has forgiven and healed us. This can encourage us to "keep going." God wants us to reach our potential to become the person He intended us to be.

It is a painful process because we live in a fallen world, and none of us is perfect, and there will continue to be difficulties, pain, and suffering. I believe there is a way to walk with God so that we can become stronger and more effective in attracting others to God. I believe the key is our individual relationship with God. Jesus never said the Christian way would be easy.

> In Matthew 16:24, *"Then Jesus said to His disciples, 'If anyone would come after me, he must deny himself and take up his cross and follow me."*

An army is made up of individuals. Each individual has a responsibility before God and will be accountable to Him on the day of judgement.

It is our choice what we do with what we have been given and what happens to us as we travel through life. God has given us free choice. Every choice we make determines the road we take. We can either opt to go God's way, which is not easy, and I will not say that it is, but the rewards are beyond measure, or we can opt to go our own way with all that entails for us. I can guarantee that if you opt for going your own way, you will never know the joy and satisfaction of a fulfilled life and of a deep relationship with the living God. Yes, we have a choice, and we alone are responsible for the choice we make.

Make no mistake, Jesus will return one day. When the gospel has been preached in the whole world, then the end will come (Matthew 24:14), and when He comes, we are told in Matthew 24:30–31:

> "At that time, the sign of the Son of Man will appear in the sky, and all the nations of the earth will mourn. They will see the Son of Man coming on the clouds of the sky, with power and great glory.
> "And He will send His angels with a loud trumpet call, and they will gather His elect from the four winds, from one end of the heavens to the other."

CHAPTER 20

My Faith

I believe that today we are no longer seen to be a Christian country. Despite this, Christianity is still a force to be reckoned with. There are many religions in this country now, but there is one very distinct aspect of Christianity that sets it apart from any other religion. The Christian religion is not "man-made."

Man-made religions are restricted to the extent of man's thinking and imagination, and they are about what man does and can do within himself/herself. It is all self-effort. The Christian faith is different in that it is a gift from God. I found that I couldn't earn my salvation in any way; it is a gift. Jesus did all the work for me by dying on the cross to bring me reconciliation with God. It was my choice as to whether I had God in my life or not.

Deep inside each one of us, I believe there is a desire to worship something or someone. We see this around us today in the hero worship of pop stars, film stars, and sports stars. We are desperate to believe in something or in someone. I have found that by having God in my life, He adds a new dimension to my way of living and my whole outlook and satisfies that inner desire to worship and have someone to look up to.

When we were known clearly as a Christian country, we had standards and values to follow. As our country has changed, it has meant that no one religion must dominate but that there should be tolerance of all beliefs. This is all very well, but I believe this has led to a lot of confusion, especially for young people. They are pulled this way and that by the different lifestyles and sets of values suggested, so they end up confused and dissatisfied.

Families are falling apart. There are very few role models in family life for young people to follow, to show them how to behave and be responsible for themselves. Many are one-parent families, which puts untold pressure upon the single parent, trying to keep a job and run a home and look after the children. As a result, children are often left to their own devices, unsupervised. One parent cannot cope properly with bringing up children on their own, however hard they try and may want to. Family values are fast disappearing; children seem to have no boundaries within which to grow up and develop safely. They show signs of insecurity in their behaviour, and some join gangs to give them a feeling of belonging. There is a lack of respect for each other, and people seem to be no longer valued. Life seems to be regarded very cheaply.

I believe that there is no better time than now for Christians to stand up for their faith. I am finding that by putting God first in my life, it changes my outlook. With God in charge, it helps me to see the world through His eyes. God shows me how much people are desperate to be loved and accepted for who they are, and I see how God's love can bring healing and wholeness to people. People's hearts are breaking and grieving — we see this on the news daily. People are fearful for their own safety and that of their family members. Normality doesn't seem to exist anymore. The world is a cruel place. I believe that as a Christian, it is my responsibility to bring God into whatever situations I find myself in so that He can make a difference.

I have found that being a Christian is not a soft option; it makes me face reality. It is tough, but the rewards are out of this world. I have found that when troubles come, in all sorts of guises, they can be used to strengthen my faith and teach me what I need to learn. God does not let anything happen to me that cannot be used to help me develop my relationship with Him. I have found the key is my reaction to the problems and difficulties I have to face. It is as I walk with God each day that I learn how to handle people and situations.

> Romans 8:28, *"And we know that in all things God works for the good of those who love Him, who have been called according to His purpose."* (My underlining.)

CHAPTER 21

Learning

One of the things I had to learn was the fact that even when I became a Christian, I still had my human side, with the ability to commit sin by thought, word and deed. The difference when I became a Christian was that I was more aware of what was right and what was wrong and the choices I had to make. This took me a while to understand.

I remember years ago when I was at work, my every word and action was under scrutiny by my colleagues. They knew I went to church and was a Christian. When I slipped up in something I said, they would come down on me very quickly, saying, "That is not the sort of thing a Christian should say." I used to feel very guilty when this happened — I was very hard on myself.

At that point, I had not learned that I was still human and prone to error. The devil is the one who makes me feel guilty; this is one of his weapons against the Christians. God convicts me of my sin, but the devil makes me feel guilty. I have learned since to accept the fact that I will make mistakes because I do not suddenly become perfect when I become a Christian. The world expects extremely high standards from Christians, and this was the pressure I was feeling at the time. I now realise that it takes a lifetime to grow in maturity with God.

God knows me better than anybody else, warts and all. There is great comfort in this and a feeling of security because He loves me unconditionally. He does not stand over me in judgement and condemnation.

I have also found that being a Christian satisfies that part of me that needs to worship someone. My worship is now directed towards God, where it should be. Being a Christian gives me a goal in life, and that is to serve God and do things for His glory and not my own. I am still a flawed human being, but as my relationship with God develops, and I allow Him to have more of me, so my sinful nature is being brought under control by God and cleansed. Although the process of becoming fully clean will not be finished until I reach heaven.

Where the things which happened to me in my past are affecting the way I live and think, God has led me along the path of healing for my inner self through His love and grace. My healings have come about through my partnership with God and my willingness to face things I would rather not, which enabled me to receive God's healing in my emotional area, to be released to become the person He has made me to be.

There are all sorts of people who claim to heal; there are all sorts of methods used to bring people healing. I have found God to be the true healer for me. There is no aftermath with God. I have found that once God has healed me, I have stayed healed, so long as I continue to live as God wants me to live and obey Him. I find it very satisfying and fulfilling to live as God wants me to live and to obey Him. It isn't drudgery to obey God. Nor is it burdensome. I find God makes life exciting - I never know what will happen next or what He wants me to do next. Having said that, God never gives me something to do which is outside my scope. I know many a time I have felt inadequate for the task He has given me, but God knows me intimately, better than I know myself, and knows what I am capable of. Where I lack anything in my work for God, He supplies what I need. The next adventure is a case in point.

I am finding that God is using me in the musical area of our church. I was approached by a friend at church and asked if I would be interested in helping to set up a singing/instrumental group and run a Taizé service as part of our church outreach.

Taizé (pronounced: tay-zay). Stephen Barany describes Taizé as a prayerful form of music known for its simple, yet rich and meditative character. Taizé as a form of music often takes the structure of a simple melody that repeats over and over and is meant to serve as a kind of musical centring prayer. I knew God wanted me involved, so I agreed. Then panic set in. Although I am musical, and I have done a lot of playing the piano and organ over the years, I have never done anything like this. I have only had an occasional opportunity to lead a choir practice at church, which, again, was a first for me and quite nerve-racking. But I believe the choir practices I took were a part of God training me for what was ahead, although I didn't know it at the time.

My friend and I started to plan and prepare for the service. We committed everything to God and prayed before we did anything. The preparations seemed to take on a momentum of their own. We prayed for the people we needed, and gradually we built up the singers and instrumentalists from our church and other churches.

The practices were my main challenge, as it was an area in which I was not overly confident. The reason for this was that when I learned to play the piano years before, I never took my Grade 3 exam. Consequently, I missed out on a lot of music theory. I have picked up a lot over the years, but I found it a bit unnerving to take these practices with people in the group who had far more musical knowledge than me. However, I persevered.

I asked God every time to help me when I took the practices, and He always enabled me to take them successfully, despite my lack of knowledge. He provided me and equipped me with what I needed. For me, this was a step of faith, and I suspect this won't be the last service I shall be involved in. God wants to use my gifts in music, and I know He will equip me with whatever I may need and encourage me to move forward in this area.

I have shared this to show you that when we commit our lives to God, He knows exactly what we are able to do and what our desires are. God alone can help us to fulfil the desires we have that are for the good of others as well as ourselves. In committing my retirement to God, He knows exactly what I need to be doing with my time, the most effective use of it, and the satisfaction gained.

This is one of the exciting aspects of being a Christian. There is always something for us to do, and as we travel along, God opens up the way for us into areas where we can grow and develop. There is always some new challenge around the corner for us.

CHAPTER 22

Power Of Prayer

I have seen that we are all on a journey together, and that's the beauty of being a part of a Christian church. We are there for each other. In the church, there are some Christians further along the path than others. It means there is a wealth of experience to draw on so that we can help each other along the road.

We hear a lot today about people's rights, but very little about people's responsibilities. I believe as a Christian, I have a very definite responsibility to other people. I have the responsibility to spread the good news of the Christian faith. People are so bombarded with words these days. I believe that living my faith each day should speak for itself to others. People should be drawn to God by seeing Him in me and other Christians as we go about our daily lives.

God has a job tailor-made for me, which only I can do, and that is where my responsibility is.

I continue to learn the importance and power of prayer. We see in the gospels how Jesus was very committed to praying to His Father in heaven. He would frequently withdraw to a quiet place and spend time with His Father in prayer. Jesus knew the importance of prayer and the strengthening He gained from these times. I am in constant conversation with my heavenly Father throughout the day. I bring Him into everything I do, chatting with Him like a friend.

It was through the power of prayer that I received God's healing.

I am a member of our prayer ministry team at church, and we always pray in pairs. We have people asking for all sorts of things. We come alongside the person in need and meet them where they are. We then pray for whatever they ask for. It is then up to God what happens next. Sometimes God will illuminate something to the person. Some people come in just to talk over something which is bothering them. With all the noise and rushing around in today's society, people are crying out to be listened to, to be heard. This, I believe, is a very important part of the ministry. We need to be available to help people along the way. At the time, it may not seem much that we pray for, but God uses whatever He wills to bring people to himself. God can see the whole picture of the person we are praying for, not just the part we can see.

> In Isaiah 55:8–9, *"For my thoughts are not your thoughts, neither are your ways my ways,"* declares the Lord.
> *"As the heavens are higher than the earth, so are my ways higher than your ways and my thoughts than your thoughts."*

I have also found that by praying regularly to God, I am continually strengthened and can live and move under His protection. We are living in dangerous times, and God's protection is very important. The devil is alive and well. He is the prince of this world, but his time of ruling the earth is limited by God. The devil has been defeated by God through the cross, and Jesus rising again from the dead.

I have also found the need to read and study God's word; this is my spiritual food to build me up and equip me. I also need the armour of God to wear for protection each day. This is my heavenly armour of protection against the enemy, the devil. I am fighting a spiritual battle, so I need spiritual equipment to protect me in the fight, as set out in Ephesians 6:10–16:

> *"Finally, be strong in the Lord and in His mighty power. Put on the full armour of God so that you can take your stand against the devil's schemes. For our struggle is not against flesh and blood, but against the rulers, against the authorities, against the powers of this dark world and against the spiritual forces of evil in the heavenly realms.*
>
> *"Therefore, put on the full armour of God, so that when the day of evil comes, you may be able to stand your ground, and after you have done everything, to stand.*
>
> *"Stand firm then, with the belt of truth buckled round your waist, with the breastplate of righteousness in place, and with your feet fitted with the readiness that comes from the gospel of peace.*

> *"In addition to all this, take up the shield of faith, with which you can extinguish all the flaming arrows of the evil one."*

I have the power of Almighty God at my disposal. God gives me all the equipment I need for the battle; it is mine for the asking. If a soldier goes to war ill-equipped, then he doesn't stand much chance of survival. God knows what I need in order to win the battle. God has won the ultimate battle, but I have skirmishes to cope with here on earth. I know I am on the side of victory. Yes, the devil can make life very difficult for me and unpleasant at times, but God only allows what He can use to teach me and strengthen me in my faith.

One of the devil's biggest cons in the world today is to convince people that he doesn't exist. As a Christian, I know that he is alive and well, but remember that he is defeated and that the power of the cross and the resurrection of Jesus is where he was defeated. That is where my victory over the devil lies.

CHAPTER 23

Trust God

Over the years, I have been learning to trust God more, and in over 40 years, I have found God to be faithful in every way. Through life's ups and downs, I have found God to be there for me, helping me, lifting me up, healing me, and helping me to move forward. His mercies are new every morning. I can have my sins forgiven each day so that I start the next day with a fresh, clean sheet. He gives me the strength to keep going, and my hope is in Him. The peace God gives is sure and steadfast, and with God, I don't know what a day may bring, but I can face it with Him. He is my guide through life's maze and my eternal hope.

> *Great is Thy faithfulness, O God my Father, there is no shadow of turning with Thee.*
>
> *Thou changest not, Thy compassions they fail not; As Thou hast been, Thou forever wilt be.*
>
> *Great is Thy faithfulness, great is Thy faithfulness.*

Morning by morning, new mercies I see; all I have needed, Thy hand hath provided. Great is Thy faithfulness, Lord unto me. Summer and winter and spring-time and harvest; sun, moon, and stars in their courses above, join with all nature in manifold witness to Thy great faithfulness, mercy, and love.

Pardon for sin, and a peace that endureth, Thine own dear presence to cheer and to guide; strength for today and bright hope for tomorrow, blessings all mine, with ten thousand beside.

Words: Thomas O Chisholm (1866–1960)

As a Christian, I have a gospel to proclaim, and the best way to do this is by the way I live my daily life. With God in charge of me, it makes a difference, and people notice that difference and want to know what it is. Is the cost too great? I don't think so. Life is hard for everyone, but through the hardships, I have God in my life with me every step of the way, and that makes a huge difference.

CHAPTER 24

Looking Back

In 1993, I didn't understand at that time the scriptures given to me by God through the counsellors because then I was living in denial of being abused. But when I did face it, I received God's healing, as mentioned earlier. It is only as I look back that I can see that the verses in Isaiah were so relevant. I had always felt isolated and didn't relate to other people, but God brought me into healing, so I was able to start to relate to people better. Because our family didn't show emotion, I kept everything bottled up. I was ashamed of who I was, but God showed me that I belonged to Him and was precious to Him. I began to build my identity in my relationship with God.

Here are a few verses which were given to me.

Isaiah 43:1b, *"…Do not fear, for I have redeemed you (from captivity); I have called you by name; you are Mine."* (AMP version)

Isaiah 43:3a, *"For I am the Lord your God, The Holy One of Israel, your Saviour."* (AMP version)

God was making me feel clean.

Hebrews 10:22, *"...let us approach [God] with a true and sincere heart in unqualified assurance of faith, having had our hearts sprinkled clean from an evil conscience, and our bodies washed with pure water.* (AMP version)

Isaiah 61:10, *"I will greatly rejoice in the Lord, My soul will exult in my God; For He has clothed me with garments of salvation, He has covered me with a robe of righteousness, As a bridegroom puts on a turban, And as a bride adorns herself with her jewels."* (AMP version)

I also had an inner hole (emotional) which was caused by a lack of fulfilment in my relationship with my father and mother. God gave me the following words from one of the counsellors:

"The walls of a broken cistern have been repaired so it can function as a fountain."

And Isaiah 58:11:
"And the Lord will continually guide you,
And satisfy your soul in scorched and dry places,
And give strength to your bones;
And you will be like a watered garden,
And like a spring of water whose waters do not fail." (AMP version)

What a wonderful promise from God. He has certainly satisfied my soul.

I was also carrying wrong responsibilities for my family, so I released each member to God and put them in His care. I have learned to put my whole family into God's care, knowing He will do a much better job than I could! I was given the following verse:

> Psalm 49:7–8:
> *"None of them can by any means redeem [either himself or] his brother,*
> *Nor give to God a ransom for him—*
> *For the ransom of his soul is too costly,*
> *And he should cease trying forever—"* (AMP version)

Over the years, God has been teaching me to learn to trust Him for everything, and I am much further along that road than I used to be.

Being a Christian is like being on a journey with God as your companion. You never stop learning, and God is always there to help, guide, heal and restore.

> In the book of Joel 2:25, we read:
> *"And I will compensate you for the years*
> *That the swarming locust has eaten,*
> *The creeping locust, the stripping locust, and the gnawing locust—*
> *My great army, which I sent among you."* (AMP version)

I feel God has more than compensated me for what I felt were lost years. He has given me lovely friends, family, and grandchildren, and He is always finding me things to do to help me develop and grow into the person He has made me to be.

In having a relationship with God, I now feel fully accepted and loved.

In 1996, God said I was to take off my masks. I would always want to appear ok, but that was being dishonest. Another work in progress has been learning not to hide behind masks anymore. It is very liberating when you can be just yourself.

> Ecclesiastes 1:9 says, *"That which has been is that which will be again, And that which has been done is that which will be done again. So there is nothing new under the sun."*

This verse tells us that "there is nothing new under the sun." Whatever state our world is in today, nothing is new about it. While men and women keep God out of their lives so the world will not be a good place to live in.

When we changed to another church, I was still working at Dorothy House. I stayed there for 10 years. I also volunteered at a local nursing home, visiting the residents and chatting with them.

In 2010, we had a new rector at the church. One of the activities the rector's wife introduced was taking Bible stories to the local primary schools. This was called "Open the Book." It entailed a team acting out the Bible stories in costume. I was able to join the team and loved every minute of it. The children responded well to our efforts. We did this for several years.

I also became a Lay Pastoral Assistant (LPA), which enabled me to visit people whom we needed to keep an eye on. It also enabled me to take Holy Communion to the housebound; we always do this in pairs.

We have been involved in helping out with our eight grandchildren – they are a real blessing, and we thank God for them. In 2014, my daughter was pregnant again, and we were looking forward to another addition to the family. The pregnancy progressed well until two weeks before the baby was due. My daughter felt that the baby wasn't moving as much as usual. I had been with her on that day and was due to go home in the evening, which I did. Later that evening, I had a phone call from my daughter to say she was in the hospital, and they couldn't find the baby's heartbeat. My husband and I immediately returned to my daughter's house, an hour and a half drive away. They told her the baby's heart had stopped, but they didn't know why. She already had two other children. My daughter had to deliver the baby on a Sunday morning. They called her Florie. It was a very distressing time. My husband and I looked after the children that weekend. The pain of losing a baby is unimaginable. At least nowadays, you are allowed to see the baby.

Over the next year, I spent most of my time at my daughter's home. I knew I should keep her company for as long as was necessary, just listening, praying quietly for guidance, and being there to offer comfort and support. There were the other two grandchildren to look after, as well, and her husband needed to talk, too. It was a very hard time for us all. We don't understand why this happened. Only God knows. Every year we visit the grave of our granddaughter, Florie; our daughter doesn't want her forgotten. Nor do we.

We were very pleased when my daughter became pregnant again. Two years later, she gave birth to a boy.

In October 2016, I asked for prayer regarding the fact that I had suffered from a great deal of anxiety since I was a child. I used to lie awake at night when my parents went out, wondering if they would come back or if they had been in an accident. I was very anxious at school, trying to cope with my schoolwork. Any change caused high anxiety as well. For the majority of my life, I had lived with this anxiety and fear as well.

After prayer, I started to question my anxiety, which had dogged me all my life. Why was I so anxious? I asked God to show me why I was so anxious. He brought to mind the scripture in Matthew 6:25:

> *"Therefore, I tell you, stop being worried or anxious (perpetually uneasy, distracted) about your life, as to what you will eat or what you will drink; nor about your body as to what you will wear. Is life not more than food and the body more than clothing?"*

> Psalm 94:19 says, *"When my anxious thoughts multiply within me, your comfort delights me."*

I then wondered about how worry or being anxious could change any situation. Well, it doesn't, I discovered. All that worry and anxiety do is wear you out; that is all it achieves. So, with God's help, I said, "I refuse to worry anymore or get so anxious that I am exhausted." I felt He made me look at my anxiety, and He asked, «What does it achieve?» I realised then that, however anxious I became, it did nothing to alter the situation. All it did was exhaust me. So, I prayed to God and said, "I refuse to get into such an anxious state again. Please help me, Lord, to overcome this. I don't want it in my life anymore. I claim your healing from my anxiety, and give it to you and thank you for taking it from me."

Because worrying and being anxious were so much a part of my life, God helped me to learn how not to get anxious and to be aware if I start to be. This took a little while, but now I don't become anxious or worried. I just remind myself that anxiety doesn't achieve anything good. I occasionally check myself to make sure I am not getting into the habit of anxiety again over things. If I feel it starting to happen, I pray and ask God to help me "not go down that road again!" My life with God is a partnership. I have my part to play, and as I work at things, I get stronger in my faith.

> The Bible says in Philippians 4:6–7: *"Do not be anxious about anything, but in everything, by prayer and petition, with thanksgiving, present your requests to God. And the peace of God, which transcends all understanding, will guard your hearts and your minds in Christ Jesus."*

Worrying doesn't change anything about the circumstances; your worry affects you and you alone.

I only learned a couple of years ago about why I failed all but three of my exams at school. I was attending a Safeguarding course and shared my experience of when I was abused. The leader of the course asked if I would mind talking with him privately after the course. I talked with him later, and he was amazed that I could share my experience so freely. I said that when God heals, He heals for good. I also said that I was no longer a "victim." So many people today are trapped by their abuse. Only God can truly free us from abuse so that we can go on to live good and fulfilling lives.

I happened to mention that I had failed all my exams, bar three. He said that was due to trauma — I never knew that! I was baffled, I have to admit because I had been put in the top stream of my secondary school, but after a year, I was put down in the next class. I wasn't a "dunce," after all! I remember feeling totally blank during the exams. Despite my poor results, I have learned.

I had to give up "Open the Book" after a few years because of not keeping well. I also had to give up singing in the choir. The reason I was feeling very unwell was due to a hiatus hernia. I had no energy and had difficulty eating and drinking.

In 2017, I went to the doctor. This had troubled me most of my life, but it had now gotten to the stage of it being really painful to eat and drink. I saw a nurse who referred me to a doctor. I had an endoscopy a few weeks later. The results showed I had 75 per cent burning all down my oesophagus, which explained the pain. No operation was possible, so tablets were prescribed. They were not at all helpful.

In desperation, I did something I don't usually do — I went onto the NHS website to see what it said. I looked up new procedures, and there was an item about keyhole surgery for hiatus hernias. I went back to the doctor. I saw a different doctor who told me I could not have an operation as it was too invasive. That puzzled me. I thought that was the point of keyhole surgery, which was meant to be far less invasive! I was quite downcast by this, but God put into my mind, "you are entitled to a second opinion."

I decided to make another appointment with a different doctor. They sent me to the doctor I originally saw, who had ordered the endoscopy. I just sat down on the chair and said to him, "Please, may I have keyhole surgery for my hiatus hernia?" He looked at me, then my notes, and said, "I don't see why not. I know the consultant who does the operation, but it is up to him to decide whether you can have it or not." I saw the consultant, and he said he would do it.

A couple of months later, I had the operation and was in hospital for 24 hours. This completely changed my health. There was a lot of soreness, which needed healing, and that took time since I was, of course, eating and drinking, but over time my oesophagus has healed, and I can eat anything now.

As I was starting to feel better than ever before, I felt ready to do something else. A lady came to our church and told us about a chaplaincy that she was running in our town. They would go out into the town in pairs and visit all the shops. They would talk to the shopkeepers and staff and let them know that they were interested in their well-being. After listening to her, I knew that this was my next step.

I have now been a town chaplain for the last few years, and it is good to get out to talk to shopkeepers and staff to encourage them in their day and let them know that we care. They appreciate our visits; we go out on Wednesdays in pairs.

I have also been able to rejoin the "Open the Book" project. We have a great team, and all of us enjoy "performing" for the children. It is a wonderful opportunity to sow the seed of God in their hearts.

Throughout my life, I have learned all I needed to know, and I will continue to learn. God has been my source of strength through it all.

God has been looking after me my whole life. He wants to be involved in our lives because of His great love for us. Yes, bad things happen to us because we live in a world that has walked away from God. The life God wants for us is a good life, a life where we can allow Him to be part of our daily lives. He cares for us so much, as my testimony shows. I have access, through prayer, to my Heavenly Father because Jesus Christ died on the cross to bear all my sins and the sins of this world. It is only through Him that we can have access to God.

But you may say, "Why does God allow all this suffering?" It is a big question, but the world is not how God intended it to be in the first place. He wanted and wants us to be in a relationship with Him, through Jesus Christ. God gave us all *free will* to choose whether to go God's way or our own. God is not responsible for all the evil happenings in the world today. It is humankind who has turned its back on God.

I gave my life to Jesus Christ at a young age (14). Life has not been easy, but God has always been there for me and helped me through my difficulties. He has never let me down. I can turn to Him at any time, so I am never alone.

I continue to play the organ occasionally, but God has got me involved in a worship band. Our rector's wife had started up a worship band, but when she retired last year, and she left, I knew God wanted me to take this on. I asked the band if they would like me to take on leading it, and they agreed.

Again, I am fully reliant on God. I am now able to play the keyboard, which I was playing in the band before our leader left. We have various instruments in the band. The majority of the players all have various grades in their instruments, so once more, I have been wholly reliant on God to help me learn the music and lead the band. God is continually stretching me to do different things. I love playing and leading worship in church, and God continues to give me opportunities to do so.

This is my life thus far. I am now 77 years old and continuing to serve God as He shows me. It doesn't matter what age we are; what is important is that we live our lives for God and do the work of His kingdom. I will continue to serve God for as long as He gives me. Life is never dull when doing His work.

I have found it is good to look back on my life. As I have done so, I have seen how God's hand has been on me, working in me and my situations to help me develop and become the person He has made me to be. We never stop learning, and so the journey will continue. I really don't know how people cope with living without God. I am thankful that He wants and longs to be part of our lives. Praise be to God!

If you have suffered abuse in your life, one of the ways that can help you is to seek professional Christian counselling. This is what I did. It helped me immensely.

Below are some useful links to Christian counselling.

Useful links for Christian Counselling:

-Harnhill Centre of Christian Healing, Driffield, Cotsworld
www.harnhillcentre.org.uk

-Reach Christian Couselling- https://www.reachuk.co.uk/
counselling/counselling-at-reach/

ABOUT THE AUTHOR

ary Joy has lived in Wiltshire since 1975, having moved there from Kent, and has celebrated 50 years of marriage to her husband, John. She has three children — two boys and a girl. They are married and have given her eight lovely grandchildren. Mary worked in the local council for 12 years and is now retired. In her spare time, she loves oil painting seascapes and portraits of her grandchildren, and they actually recognise themselves in them!

Mary plays the organ and the keyboard in her church band. She is also a Lay Pastoral Assistant and is part of the "Open the Book" team in Wiltshire, which performs Bible stories in schools.

Printed in Great Britain
by Amazon

21593743R00058